D0251213

I'd like to dedicate this book to all of the girls
who have broken my heart over the years...
which is none! ha!
ha!
ha!

Copyright © 2007 by Todd Harris Goldman

All rights reserved. No portion of this book may be reproduced—mechanically,
electronically, or by any other means, including photocopying—without
written permission of the publisher. Published simultaneously in
Canada by Thomas Allen & Son Limited.

Library of Congress Cataloging-in-Publication Data is available.

ISBN-13: 978-0-7611-4851-7

Workman books are available at special discounts when purchased in bulk
for premiums and sales promotions as well as for fund-raising or educational use.
Special editions or book excerpts also can be created to specification. For
details, contact the Special Sales Director at the address below.

Design by Todd Harris Goldman

Workman Publishing Company, Inc.
225 Varick Street
New York, NY 10014-4381
www.workman.com

Printed in China
First printing October 2007

10 9 8 7 6 5 4 3 2 1

INTRO

Girls. I don't get them. I don't understand them or have the slightest clue about what makes them tick. Therefore I have decided to write a book about them. Makes perfectly good sense to me. Call it therapy, call it stupidity, call it a pathetic, desperate cry for help . . . any way I look at it, the truth seems fairly obvious:

Girls are weirdos!

hee! hee!

bird poop

ME

ACCESSORIZING

Why do you girls need so many damn accessories? Rings, necklaces, watches, bracelets, hairclips, hats, bags, belts, scarves, blah, blah, blah. You even have accessories for your accessories ... like stupid charm bracelets! Isn't the bracelet already an accessory? Pretty stupid, if you ask me.

oooh a charm bracelet, how charming!

4

ALL DRESSED UP
AND NOWHERE TO GO

Why do girls get all dressed up for no reason?
I have seen girls with a full face of makeup and
high heels at the gym. Stop pretending you're
important and have somewhere to be. Unless you're
Miss America, there's really no need to get all
dolled up to go grocery shopping.

tiara

THE GROCERY STORE

SALE

BAD BOYS

Why is it that girls seem to prefer bad boys to nice ones? Don't you realize that with a little time and patience nice boys will end up treating you just as badly as the bad boys do? Geez!

BAD HAIR DAY

Why do girls get so upset over a bad hair day?
I mean, come on, it's only temporary! It will be
fine tomorrow, ladies. You should be grateful
you even have hair, even though half your hair
is fake anyway! I would be more concerned with a
bad face day or a bad body day. Those are more
permanent and can only be fixed with
plastic surgery.

BFF

I think this should stand for "best friends for now," and girls should admit to changing their BFFs like I change my underwear, which is once a week. At least that would be honest. Let's face it, girls: You aren't always that loyal to your BFFs. Like, on the one hand you'll be all "I love you, you're SO my BFF" to your BFF's face, but if a guy you like so much as looks at your BFF, you'll say awful things behind her back to all your other friends. Or maybe BFF should stand for "backstabbing friends forever"?

BLONDES, BRUNETTES, & REDHEADS

BLONDES: Do blondes really have more fun? Do bears poop in the woods? Of course they do. If you soaked your head in bleach and killed half your brain cells just to look like a Barbie doll, you'd be a lot of fun, too. Look at all the fun Paris Hilton, Britney Spears, and ~~Anna Nicole Smith~~ are having. —OOPS

BRUNETTES: Well, if blondes are the dumb ones, then brunettes must be the smart ones. I mean, look at Katie Holmes: She's so smart she joined a cult.

REDHEADS: Who cares!

BOY BANDS

Why do all girls go through a Boy Band phase?
It can't be for the music! Sure, these guys start
out cute enough, I guess, but you know they all
end up working as security guards or, even worse,
as sweaty contestants on Dancing with the Stars.
Ah, maybe I'm just bitter because I got cut
at the New Kids on the Block tryouts!
Well, at least I'm not bald now, Donnie!

BUG GIRL

What is with oversize sunglasses? Why do you girls want to look like giant flies? If you want to keep the sun out of your eyes, why don't you just put a paper bag over your head? At least paper bags are free. These oversize space goggles cost upwards of $300. And they make you look ridiculous!

✳ Also, BTW, when you wear them, we can't see your fake contacts.

CANDLELIGHT DINNERS

Who said candlelight dinners are romantic?
Who wants to eat in the dark?
I want to see my T-bone steak, thank you very
much. That's probably why Thomas Edison invented
the light bulb: He was sick of having candlelight
dinners with his wife. Girls, unless you live in
a cave or you're allergic to light, try
turning on the light switch.
It's called electricity.

CATFIGHTS

There's nothing better than a good old-fashioned catfight. Two chicks fighting over nothing. It even beats Portuguese slap-fighting and midget pudding wrestling. Where else can you see two girls clawing each other's eyes out over a piece of gum? But let's not confuse this with COW FIGHTS where two fat girls are fighting over a piece of meatloaf. This, not so much fun to watch.

CHEERLEADERS

These are attention-seeking snobs who can't spell
except when forming a pyramid. Hey, girlies:
We know who you are! The polyester skirt
ensembles give it away, so stop carrying the
pom-poms wherever you go already!
Gimme a B-I-M-B-O! What does it spell?

GO TEAM!

YAY!

2-4-6-8
i'm a really
easy date!
YAY!

Wait, quick form a pyramid!

CHICK FLICKS

There isn't anything that I love more than sitting home on a Saturday night, spooning under a blanket with my girlfriend, watching a chick flick. I love to cry and be held while my true, deep emotions exude from my heart. Bridget Jones's Diary, Pretty Woman, The Notebook, and Serendipity. Gosh, life is so beautiful!

CHOCOLATE

The yummiest, tastiest, bestest treat in the whole wide world. It makes you happy and makes all your problems go away. It's even better than sex. But it also makes you fat and gives you pimples. Which means you won't be having much sex anyway, so I guess it all evens out!

← ZITS

CLIQUES

Every girl falls into one of these cliques:

THE PREPPIES: the upper-class snobs and cheerleaders who think they're better than everyone else.

THE JOCKS: the future gym teacher lesbians.

THE NERDS: the geeky, dorky, smart girls with glasses and braces who you cheat off of.

THE GANGSTAS: the white girls who wear oversize clothes, listen to rap music, and think they're black.

the preppies

the jocks

the nerds

the gangstas

the hotties

THE HOTTIES: the stripper wannabes and weekend bikini and wet T-shirt contestants.

THE HIPPIES: the sandal-wearing, granola-eating, hairy-legged pale girls who carpool to school to save the environment.

THE MODELS: the anorexic chicks who eat a grape and then throw it up.

THE GOTHS: the girls who shop at Hot Topic and think that wearing black makes them look dark and evil.

THE ARTSY FARTSIES: the girls who sit under the trees at lunch and write poems about their feelings.

the
hippies

the
models

the
goths

the artsy
fartsies

CRUSHES

I remember my first crush. It was on my 4th grade teacher, Miss Howie. It was sad. I really wanted to marry her, but I was ten and she was thirty. I thought we could make it work, but she saw otherwise. I still have my 4th grade class photo in my room, and I'm sure she still has my drawing of us on our wedding day on her refrigerator. Oops, my mistake, they don't allow fridge magnets in nursing homes. ☺

* Remember, girls, when boys have crushes on you, they like to pull your hair. The harder they pull, the more they like you!

DATING

I don't understand dating today! Nowadays it's all about meeting online, having the girl sneak out of her window, making out after the first five minutes, hanging out at the mall, and having text-messaged sex. Why can't we just go back to the caveman days? Everything was much simpler back then...

me like woman!

← DINOSAUR

CAVEMAN →

21

DIAMONDS

Dictionary definition is...

—n: A pure, or nearly pure, extremely hard form of carbon, naturally crystallized in the isometric system.

—n: A very expensive rock often used in rings, necklaces, and bracelets.

My definition is...

—n: A form of currency that boys use to trade with girls for sex.

* Also, why are diamonds a girl's best friend? Dogs are man's best friends, which makes perfectly good sense to me. But being ~~BFF~~ with a rock is kinda weird!

DIET

A four-letter word that starts with eating healthy and going to the gym and ends with sneaking chocolate cake into your bed. It's funny that girls assume anything with the word "diet" or "organic" or "low-fat" in it is healthy and therefore proceed to consume twice as much. "I would like 8 tofuburgers, 10 large zero-transfat fries, 24 farm-raised chicken nuggets, 5 organic apple pies, 4 low-fat caramel sundaes, and a diet soda please . . ."

it's ok, i'm on a diet!

23

DOES THIS DRESS MAKE ME LOOK FAT?

You already know the answer, don't you? You're just looking for someone to be mad at, that's all. So if I tell you the truth, you get pissed at me. And if I lie, you get even more pissed at me. I can't win either way! So I'm going to answer you straight-up once and for all (and I'm doing this for every guy who's ever been tortured by this same stupid question):

YES, THAT DRESS MAKES YOU LOOK FAT!

You're not skinny enough to pull it off!

SPANDEX IS A PRIVILEGE, NOT A RIGHT!

Next question...

DRAMA QUEENS

"OMG I look so fat today, I must have gained 100 pounds, I'm never eating again!"
"Ryan hasn't called me in 15 minutes, he's probably cheating on me, I think I'm going to die." "My cell phone bill is so high this month I'm probably going to have to declare bankruptcy and get a job." "I'm so never leaving the house again, I have a huge zit the size of Mt. Everest on my chin."

If this is you, please SHUT UP. No one cares!

EAT SOMETHING ALREADY

Okay, girls, here's a lesson you need to learn: Food, which is good for you, should be eaten, digested, then pooped out, all in one continuous railroad track of happy digestion and nutrition. If you eat, then puke, the train derails. If you never eat anything, the train can't leave the station. Just because we like you skinny and hot doesn't mean it's okay to stick your finger down your throat.

BLAAA!

NO!

EWW! BUGS!

Why are girls afraid of bugs? You are 100,000 times bigger than they are. Bugs should be afraid of you with all that makeup and bug spray you call perfume on. If you're going to be afraid of something, be afraid of something really scary, like a dinosaur, or a Bigfoot, or someone who just looks like a bug. Celine Dion, for instance: Now THAT is scary!

CELINE DION

blah blah, titanic song... blah blah

ahhhh! what is that horrible creature? I think it's Canadian!

bugs

EX-BOYFRIENDS

Girls, keep your ex-boyfriend stories to yourselves. Remember, the prefix "ex" means former, no longer, used to be... let's keep it that way. We don't need to hear how he broke your heart, and how cute and romantic he was. If he was so great, why is he your ex? Also, we don't need to see pictures of him either (unless he's in a Speedo, then that's okay!). Thanks!

EX-BOYFRIEND

FAKE BOOBS

I am 100% for fake boobies! As well as breasts, jugs, knockers, hooters, fun bags, or tatas, as some people like to call them. Whatever the name, I think it looks completely natural to have giant watermelons popping out of your shirt. Besides, they look and feel so real most guys can't tell the difference anyways ...especially the basketball kind!

FAKE EYELASHES

Nothing is sexier than a girl with thick black 3-inch plastic rods coming out of her eyes. It looks like a tarantula got stuck on its back and is kicking its legs in the air. Why do girls go through the torture of gluing those things on? I guess it's some sort of contraption to capture food for the eye ...like a Venus flytrap.

FAKE 'N' BAKE

There is nothing less attractive than a girl who looks like a leather handbag and glows in the dark. Not that I have anything against the color orange, I just don't like it as the color of your skin. Leave that for oranges, pumpkins, carrots, sweet potatoes, highlighters, the Cleveland Browns, and traffic cones, please. I actually once dated a girl who was shaped like a traffic cone, but at least her skin wasn't orange!

OK!

NOT OK!

FAKE NON-EATERS

I don't understand girls who don't eat in front of other people. They order a small salad and have one bite. "That crouton sure was filling. I'm stuffed!" But when they get home, they pig out on a gallon of cookie dough ice cream. I can understand not wanting to pick and eat your boogers in front of someone, that's not very ladylike, but what's wrong with a salad? Think how the salad feels: Every time a girl doesn't finish her salad . . . God kills a carrot. 😞

on a hot date:

at home after date

FIRST KISS

I love that awkward feeling of having butterflies in my stomach when I'm about to kiss someone for the very first time. This is different from eating butterflies because I like the taste of bugs, but that's a whole other topic. Your eyes are closed, your hands are shaking, you're sweating profusely, and your heart is racing . . . it's kind of the same feeling you get when you're about to take a giant dump. I love that feeling!

FLIRTING

Commonly known as a flirt or a tease. This is when a girl is overly friendly and leads a boy on with no intention of putting out. Some examples are: blowing kisses, winking, touching, tickling, playing footsies, head butting, wedgies, and free lap dances.
Girls, please quit the games!

* Note: This is different than FOREPLAY, which is what happens right before sex when a guy fantasizes that four naked girls are playing charades with him.

FLOWERS

Also known as the "get out of jail free" card. Guys love flowers! I mean guys love the power of flowers. We can totally get in a fight, cheat on our girlfriend, run over her dog, and accidentally sleep with her best friend . . . and everything will be okay. Why? Because we sent her flowers. A dozen smelly little weeds that die in a week just saved our ass.

ooh flowers!!! i forgive you for killing Fluffy!

I love flowers.

SUCKER!

GEEKS

Face it, geeky girls are sexy. Thick, horn-rimmed glasses, orthopedic shoes, SpongeBob backpack, the occasional back brace and headgear...everything about geeky girls oozes sex appeal. Chess is a way sexier sport than field hockey—have you seen some of those goalies? The fact that they're smarter than me turns me on, too. Having a girl tell me that William Howard Taft was our 27th president is like foreplay to me.

hey sexy! LOOKIN' GOOD!

i love you, Todd!

37

GIRLS' NIGHT OUT

This is when a group of girlfriends go out on a bonding bitch session to complain about everything wrong with their lives. Their boyfriends, their classes, their boyfriends, their jobs, their boyfriends, etc. They get obnoxiously drunk, go to male strip clubs, and usually end up having meaningless sex with a stranger. This is different from BOYS' NIGHT OUT, where guys get together to read poetry, drink sparkling water, play Scrabble, chat about celebrity hook-ups, and discuss fashion trends.

i hate my boss, she's such a bitch!

my boyfriend SUCKS!

can you believe who Paris is dating?

GIRLY MAGAZINES

Seventeen, Vogue, Cosmo, Teen Queen, whatever...
they're all the same. They're basically just
instruction manuals telling girls how to dress
to attract guys, what kind of guys to date, how
to get rid of unwanted zits so guys will sleep with
you, and how to stay under 90 pounds so guys will
find you hot. Guys like them because, duh, they're
full of articles on guys (e.g., how to drive a guy
crazy in bed), so it drives home the point that
making us happy is really what it's all about.
Like getting fake boobies!

GYM BUNNIES

These are the super-fake, overly buff girls who wear tight leotards and have big fake boobs. These she-men always make sure that everyone in the gym has a good view of their hyper-hard butts. They're usually blonde with hair extensions and have their tans airbrushed on to accentuate their six-packs. Come to think of it, I need to renew my gym membership.

* Caution: Guys, if a girl can bench-press more than you...she might not really be a girl! :)

HAIR EXTENSIONS

Why do girls weave hair from a horse's rear end to their heads? I think that's taking the term "ponytail" a little too far, don't you? Instead, why not go down to the highway and pick up some roadkill? What's wrong with a little opossum or squirrel hair? And just think, with a skunk you wouldn't have to put streaks in your hair, either.

that's HOT!

HOT AND FRESH FROM THE OVEN

Mmmmm! I sure do like muffins, hot and fresh from the oven. But there is one type of muffin I can do without...the MUFFIN TOP. You've seen them, huge chunks of flesh bulging out over a girl's tight pants, gasping for air. This strange spillover effect is the cause of many stomachaches and traffic accidents. Ladies, if you're going to wear tight pants and a small top so your entire midriff flops over your belt, please, at least give us a warning . . . like one of those WIDE LOAD signs you see on trucks. At least we'll know to get out of your way.

I CAN TELL YOUR BAG IS FAKE

Why do girls buy fake designer handbags? Do they think they're fooling anyone? They might as well be carrying a trash bag with handwritten logos on it. I especially like the really bad fakes from China and Korea where the logo is misspelled—as if that's actually going to fool someone! "Oh, hey, do you like my PRABBA bag?" Or "Look, I'm rich. Here's my GUCCIE bag." Or maybe you carry these obvious fake bags to distract us from your other fake things...like your boobs and hair! Yeah, that's probably it.

I LIKE CLOWNS

Once I was at the mall and I went up to this lady and asked her to make me a balloon animal. An elephant, to be exact. She looked at me like I was crazy. I said: "Lady, where is your red nose and funny hat and big shoes?" She hit me with her bag and walked away. Girls, the moral to my story is simple...if you wear too much makeup you might get mistaken for a clown. So make sure you have plenty of balloons in your pocket.

balloon

I LOVE YOU!

The three most ~~beautiful~~ HORRIBLE words in the world!

I'M CONFUSED

What is a tampon? What is the difference between a pad and a tampon? Why a string? Is this so you find your way back? Why not just use breadcrumbs? My mom always told me to use Bounty when I made a mess, it's the quicker picker-upper. Never, after spilling my tomato juice on the counter, did she hand me a tampon. Another thing: Why are they shaped so weird? Like cardboard torpedoes! I heard that some are even made of pearls! That must be expensive! Why do you make us guys pick them up for you at the store? Ladies, please leave us alone when it comes to tampons—they scare us.

I'M LIKE A MODEL!

Girls, just because you spent money on some photos at Glamour Shots doesn't mean you're a model. If that's the case, then every girl in my high school yearbook was a model, too. And believe you me, Lucinda Green was no model . . . she could stop traffic with that mug. So please, girls, unless you're doing fashion runway shows in Paris or gracing the pages of Vogue and Cosmo, please stop telling us you're a model. Because you're not!

look, i'm a model!

paparazzi

LIP GLOSS

This is the shiny, sticky crap girls put on their lips. We know it's not for kissing because most girls are prudes. So I'm not sure if it's to attract flies, reflect sunlight to recharge their solar-powered vibrators, or to guide airplanes in for landing. Also, now that we're on the subject of lips, what's with this whole collagen craze? Is it true you girls really stick needles in your lips just to make yourselves look like a duck? Or is it that you want a bigger target for your lip gloss? That's just stupid.

LITTLE DOGS

What's the point of having a dog that you can accidentally step on? Isn't that why God created hamsters? And, by the way, that stupid yappy little furball of yours is pooping and peeing all over your house! Do you think its shit doesn't stink just because you painted its toenails pink? And what's with sticking your dog in a purse and carrying it around town all day? How would you like it if I shoved you in a bag and dragged you to the mall for the Groundhog Day sale at the Gap?

YAP YAP YAP YAP YAP YAP YAP YAP YAP YAP YAP YAP YAP YAP YAP YAP YAP YAP YAP YAP

MANIS AND PEDIS

Please explain to me what is so relaxing about sitting in a chair having someone poke at your fingers and toes with sharp metal tools while Mandarin wedding music is playing in the background? I think I'd rather be tortured in a Turkish prison. Plus, I am perfectly happy with my cuticle bed, thank you very much. What do you think holds down my fingernails and toenails?

MOUSTACHES

Ladies, guys don't like it when you look like their Uncle Nick! We also don't like being pricked in the face when we try to kiss you. Wax that caterpillar! Moustaches are for guys, just like changing diapers, washing dishes, doing laundry, cooking, and cleaning are for girls.

ONE NIGHT STAND

Despite what you say,
I know every girl has had at least
one night stand.

ONE
NIGHT
STAND

ONLINE DATING

Girls, stop lying about yourself online, we're onto your scam.
Hi, I'm SEXBUNNY69, let's chat sometime...

This is what SEXBUNNY69 says:
My name is Bunny, I'm 17,
5' 10", 100 lbs., 34 C, blonde
hair and blue eyes. I like
unicorns, skinny-dipping,
glitter, and making out.

BUNNY ←

BERTHA ↙

This is what SEXBUNNY69 means:
My name is Bertha, I'm 42,
4' 6", 350 lbs., 48 FF, patchy
red hair, and only one eye.
I like buffets, Twinkies,
walruses, bench pressing, and
collecting roach droppings.

* Note: MySpace is a great place
to stalk—I mean meet—girls.

PARTY FRIEND

Every girl has a party friend, aka slut. We're not talking about the girl wearing a party hat at Chuck E. Cheese's who's helping some little kid blow out their birthday candles. No. I'm talking about the scantily dressed girl who parties almost every night of the week. She is either at a club or frat party drinking, doing drugs, and having sex with random guys. More often than not, she wakes up in the morning with a note duct-taped to her forehead saying "thanks for the good time."

PDA

Ahh, Public Displays of Affection, holding hands, cuddling, snuggling, hugging, spooning, whispering sweet nothings in each other's ears, how cute...PUKE!!!! Guys hate this crap! Why do you make us do this? Why do you torture us and grab our arm while we're walking, are you going to fall down or something? Did you forget how to walk? I think you do this intentionally to embarrass us, to mark your territory like a dog peeing on a tree. That's okay, when you're sleeping, we stick your toothbrush in the toilet

NO! HELP!

YUCK!

let's cuddle!

* but remember, girls: spooning sometimes leads to forking!

PERIOD. END OF STORY.

The monthly bill, the crimson tide, on the rag, Aunt Flo, the redheaded stepchild: Whatever the name, they all mean the same thing...eww! Gross! Guys, take my advice: When a girl has her period ... RUN! Run as fast as you can and don't look back! Take a week's vacation, come back, and hopefully the mess will all be cleaned up by then.

AAH! RUN!

eww! tampon!

✶ Also, let's not confuse this with PMS, aka Psychotic Mood Swings. This is when girls get really pissed off that they're girls in the first place. I can't say I blame them. If I knew my wiener was going to leak ketchup every month for the rest of my life, I'd be pissed off too.

57

PIERCINGS AND TATTOOS

The art of shoving pieces of metal through your body. Tongue, lip, nose, belly button, ears, eyebrows, eyelids, nipples, and you know where ...ouch! Girls, I don't get it! Is it for the free cable or do you think it's cool to look like an African warrior? If you're going to put holes in your body, why don't you use picture hooks instead? This way you can display your family photos on your body instead of tattooing them on.

I ♥ TODD

*Speaking of tattoos, what's with all the ink, huh?
You look like a newspaper. Is it really necessary to put your boyfriend's name on your arm? Is it so you don't call out the wrong name during sex?

PINK

Why is everything pink? What is the fascination with the color pink? Girls go crazy for it. I don't get it. Pink, pink, pink, pink, pink, pink, pink! Their cell phones and bedsheets, all pink. Their purses, shoes, and cars, what else? Pink. Even their dogs are pink! Everything is freakin' pink! That's why I made the cover of this book pink, by the way, because I knew that, despite the title, girls were going to buy it. . . . Why? Because it's PINK!

PLASTIC SURGERY

This is where ugly girls have the option of spending tons of money to make themselves pretty by inserting silicone and plastic into their bodies. I say, why bother? You're still butt-ugly, but now it's probably because you really do have a piece of your butt surgically appended to your face. That's what they mean by cheek implants, you know!

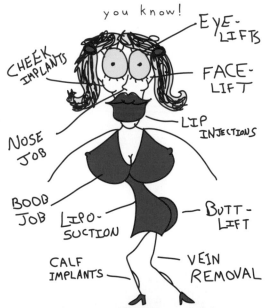

PLUCKERS

I hate pluckers! You know those girls who have like six eyebrow hairs in a perfect straight line above each eye? People with alopecia have thicker eyebrows. I also hate those penciled-on eyebrows. Are you trying to look like a clown? I hear some girls even get them tattooed on. Ouch! I wonder if moms who pluck their eyebrows are called "mother pluckers."

tweezers 61

PROM

This is where the not-so-hot chicks in high school get to put on fancy dresses and pretend they're cool, ride in limos, be seen with the popular kids, dance the night away to Madonna and Kool and the Gang, drink spiked punch, and go on the one and only date they'll ever have. And if they're lucky, they lose their virginity to some drunk guy like me who doesn't even know their name, while the dork who took them to the prom and spent money on the corsage is playing Dungeons & Dragons with his equally dweeby friends in the men's room.

not-so-hot chick

the dork

me, the drunk guy

PUSH-UP BRAS

I just discovered this scam. Your boobs aren't that big! It's all a lie. You're 80% bra. I even heard there are some filled with water. Little water balloons sewn into fabric to make guys think that girls have boobs. If you really cared all that much, you'd just go and have a boob job (see page 60). At least THOSE are real!

BEFORE

AFTER

* I would like to personally take this opportunity to thank Victoria's Secret. You have helped me through many lonely nights. I don't know your secret, and I don't care; just keep sending me free catalogs in the mail.

63

SHOES

Why do girls have so damn many pairs of shoes?
Is there some secret contest guys don't know
about? The one with the most shoes wins?
Also, when they find a pair of shoes they like,
why do they need them in every color?
They only have two feet like everyone else
(except one-legged people, they only have one
foot). Correct me if I'm wrong, but logic
tells me girls only need one pair of shoes.

SHOPPING

I don't get girls' obsession with shopping!
It doesn't matter what they're buying or whether
they already have it...they have to have it again.
And again, and again, and again!
Shoes, clothing, jewelry, makeup, Twinkies, gum,
Band-Aids, rat poison, peanut butter, paper
clips, doggie poop bags, anything...They must have
everything! And if it's on sale, they need twice
as much...which kind of defeats the purpose,
if you ask me.

SILENT TREATMENT

Oooh, you're not talking to me! Thanks, I can use the break. The phone calls every 15 minutes asking me where I am, and what I'm doing, and who I'm with, were getting kind of annoying. So basically I'm a huge fan of the silent treatment and wish you girls used it more often.

SKINNY JEANS

Skinny jeans are hot...on SKINNY girls!
Hello, Earth to Pudgie: If your waist size is
twice your age and you can't see your feet, then
you probably shouldn't be wearing skinny jeans.
Just because they're called "skinny" jeans doesn't
mean they'll make you look skinny! Or do you
think wearing glasses makes you look smarter, too?

AIR!
i need AIR!

SMART vs. DUMB GIRLS

Girls, here's the truth: Guys don't like smart girls. We like dumb girls—the dumber the better. So don't bother learning math or how to read. It's a waste of time! Just know how to make yourselves look cute when we go out. That's all the smarts required. And how to make a good sandwich. We like sandwiches.

good, girlie! now fetch!

here's your sanwech!

SORORITIES

This is what you get when you put 100 cackling hens in a house, give them 3 Greek letters so they can sew them on every article of clothing they own, sing stupid songs, sleep with frat boys, call each other "sisters," plan ridiculous date functions and other meaningless college get-togethers, and pig out just to gain 25 pounds so nobody recognizes them when they go home for the summer. Oooh, congratulations, you're a legacy, please sign here!

♪ we're the girls of XXX.
we like to sleep around,
we each gained 25 pounds,
we like frat boys,
and sex toys! ♪

TEEN IDOLS

Britney Spears, Lindsay Lohan, Paris Hilton, Nicole Richie? Let's get serious now! When did doing drugs, getting drunk, and sleeping around become traits to idolize? Girls should look up to a real role model like Richard Simmons. Think about it. He's got a great body, makes "the perm" look cool again, brought back short shorts, and makes fat people feel good about themselves. Now that's a poster I want hanging in my room!

THE GIRL SQUAD

The entourage, the self-paparazzi, and the mall rats. Maybe girls have read about the theory that there's power in numbers, and that's why they like to travel in packs like herds of buffalo wandering the Great Plains. And, weirdly enough, no matter how many girls in a pack, it always breaks down to a 1:2:1 ratio. That is, one super-hot chick, two average chicks, and one MUF (the Mandatory Ugly Friend).

These girl packs wander the malls hunting for boys, screaming, shopping, and eating ice cream.

1:2:1

HOT CHICK

AVERAGE CHICKS

MUF

THE MUF

Speaking of MUFs, why do pretty girls always seem to have one? Is it to make themselves look prettier? Is it because they think they need a bodyguard? It does seem like you always have to get past the MUF to get to the hottie. You have to pretend to be interested in whatever the ogre's saying, and laugh at her stupid jokes, just to get close to the target. But this hardly ever works!

Most of the time you get stuck talking to the MUF all night long while the hottie trots away. This really sucks!

TICK TICK TICK

What's that ticking sound? Is that the oven timer?
Oh no, it's your BABY-MAKER clock. Excuse me,
I have a plane to catch.

UNDIES

I'm pretty sure I speak for all guys here when I say that guys can't stand when girls wear thongs. A tiny strip of fabric barely covering a chick's butt crack so her entire backyard can be seen... that's disgusting. Ladies, guys want to leave a little something to the imagination, which is why we are huge fans of...

GRANNY PANTIES!

* Note: Granny panties are hot. Grannies in panties: <u>not</u> so hot.

* Remember: We wear tighty whities for you, because we know you think it's sexy!

UP, DOWN, UP, DOWN

The never-ending battle of the toilet seat.
As a kid growing up and sharing a bathroom with
my sister, nothing was more enjoyable than hearing
her scream as she sat down in my pee. I would
hide behind the closet door and wait for the
exciting moment to unfold, as my pee droplets
glistened in the sun. Girls, the moral to this
story is simple...don't put down the toilet seat
or we will pee on it! ☺

WALK OF SHAME

We have all seen her: the girl with the messy hair, runny makeup, wearing the same clothes she wore the night before, stumbling to her car, shoes in hand, purse dragging behind on the ground, hurrying home to take a shower after her embarrassing one-night stand. It just sucks when it's your best friend's mom.

WHAT ARE WE?

Apparently, relationship status is very important to girls. It's even a criteria on MySpace! Single or In A Relationship? That's the big question. Are we boyfriend and girlfriend or are we just friends? Are we exclusive or can we date other people? Then when you finally decide that we are boyfriend/girlfriend, the next day you don't want a boyfriend anymore.

This really confuses me.

My head hurts, who cares, let's just cuddle.

WHAT'S THIS CRAP ON TV?

The OC, Laguna Beach, The Hills...what is this garbage? What happened to good quality programming and real acting like they had in the good old days of Buffy the Vampire Slayer, Beverly Hills 90210, and Charmed? When Tori Spelling got snubbed by the Emmy Awards despite her brilliant performance as Donna Martin in the episode "Finally Someone Thinks I'm Attractive," I wept for almost a week straight. Now THAT was television at its greatest.

I LOVE YOU, David Silver!

Tori Spelling, Yuck!

WHERE TO MEET BOYS

We've all heard the best place to meet someone is at the library or the grocery store, but have you seen the people that hang out at the library? Unless you're looking for someone who can solve a Rubik's Cube backwards, my advice is to try a more logical place. Like a sperm bank, for instance. Think about it—your only competition is a bunch of dated girly magazines, and you'll know for sure the guy's fertile (see TICK TICK TICK on page 73 to know why that's important). What more could you ask for?

wee!

SPERM BANK

baby

WHO IS THIS WEIRD GIRL?

I was just thinking...seeing that my mom is a girl, and chances are that one day I'm probably going to marry a girl...shoot, maybe I'll even have a daughter! Hmm, maybe girls aren't that bad after all? I mean, without girls we wouldn't be able to procreate. And who would do my laundry and who would I have sex with? That would be the end of civilization and then the bugs would take over the world.

Nah, what am I talking about...

MY MOM

GIRLS

ARE

WEIRDOS!

but they smell pretty.

the end.

sorry, mom.

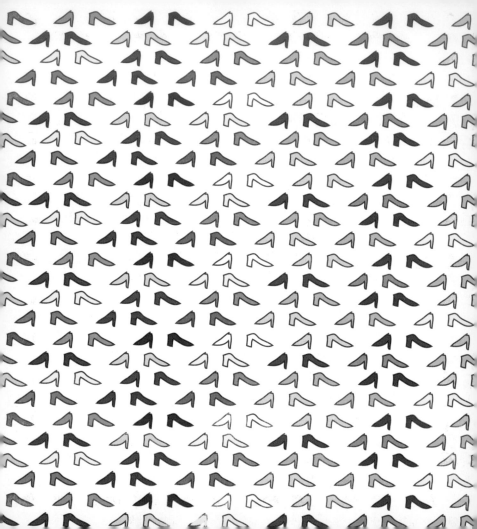